JAMES HIPKISS

UNARMED COMBAT

BY

JAMES HIPKISS
(British Ju-Jitsu Champion)

First Impression .	February, 1941
Second Impression .	February, 1941
First "Popular" Edition	March, 1941

The Naval & Military Press Ltd

Published by

The Naval & Military Press Ltd

Unit 5 Riverside, Brambleside
Bellbrook Industrial Estate
Uckfield, East Sussex
TN22 1QQ England

Tel: +44 (0)1825 749494

www.naval-military-press.com
www.nmarchive.com

CONTENTS

INTRODUCTORY

There are now available many books dealing with the new methods of warfare which have been developed during the Second Great War. But until the publication of this booklet none has attempted to give an adequate exposition of the art of Unarmed Combat—the art of fighting, and winning, without weapons.

Now, no one will suggest that an unarmed man has a great deal of chance against an enemy armed with a tommy gun or a basket of hand-grenades. In such circumstances the likelihood of the survival of the unarmed one would depend, perhaps, more on his fleetness of foot than upon the information to be gleaned from these pages. But an enemy is not necessarily always heavily armed : he may, for the moment, not be within reach of his weapons : ammunition sometimes runs out. And in such case, victory in the little spot of bother that arises when enemies meet is very certainly going not to the bigger man, not to the stronger man, not even to the most agile man, but to the man who knows most about the principles of Unarmed Combat.

The principles at the root of the art of Unarmed Combat are largely those of ju-jitsu (judo), and the various other styles of wrestling and self-defence devices. That their importance is now fully recognised by the Government is shown by the fact that considerable numbers of members of the fighting services are now being especially trained in "Unarmed Combat" so that they, in turn, may instruct the rest of us. For, while no one imagines for a moment that we are going to tackle the enemy with nothing but our bare hands if we can get anything else into them, yet the authorities do now realise that knowledge of the principles of Unarmed Combat

is an invaluable adjunct to the fighting strength of a people,
an inestimably useful addition to a people's defensive (and
offensive) equipment.

But the matter goes deeper than that. Knowledge of the
art of antagonistics (as Unarmed Combat is sometimes
described) gives self-confidence and self-reliance to those
who possess it : and the practice of the art, in a friendly
way between comrades, aids physical fitness and adds to the
suppleness of the whole organism, mental and physical.
Even though one may never have to use the principles of
Unarmed Combat in war, they constitute an asset of worth
throughout the whole of one's life.

In this country the people qualified to furnish a concise
and lucid exposition of the art of Unarmed Combat are few.
Among the few is Mr. James Hipkiss, British Ju-Jitsu
Champion and (among many other activities at the present
time) Headquarters Instructor in Unarmed Combat to Birming-
ham's Home Guard. In this booklet Mr. Hipkiss has outlined
with an admirable lucidity that cannot fail to be understood
by everybody, aided as his words are by some most graphic
illustrations, practically everything that it is possible to teach
of the art of Unarmed Combat. It is an exposition complete
and clear.

It may be added, of course, that knowledge of Unarmed
Combat will be acquired most rapidly if this booklet is used
in conjunction with practical physical instruction : even so,
however, there are few people who could fail to learn a great
deal of the art of self-defence and intelligent attack from the
book alone—so crystally clear are the various movements
described.

CHAPTER I

At the basis of the art of acquiring the skill necessary to overcome an antagonist there is one outstanding principle. Briefly that principle is this :

" A MAN WITHOUT BODY BALANCE HAS NO STRENGTH."

That is to say that a man whose body is not properly poised, whose body is not perfectly balanced, not merely cannot utilise his strength but can have it exerted against himself and to the benefit of his antagonist.

In any struggle between men who, being unarmed, must rely upon their own muscular exertions, it is absolutely essential that the man who wills to win must make certain that it is *he* who remains in possession of the poise, the body balance, that will enable him to use to the full what strength he has : it is also essential that he should endeavour, by unbalancing his adversary, to render that adversary's strength abortive.

How is body balance achieved and maintained ? Body balance depends entirely upon the position of the feet, which must at all times be kept the *same distance apart as one's shoulders are wide*. So that when one foot is moved, the other instantly follows it to resume the first position. It must be realised that your feet must never be stretched wide apart, nor must they be brought close together.

If, for example, you step backwards with, say, your left foot, the right foot is rapidly snatched after it, to assume the fundamental or natural stance, a stance in line with your shoulders and the same distance apart.

Start your first practice then, by moving about the floor, first sliding one foot back and drawing the other after it quickly, until, no matter how you move, you can always stop instantly *in balance* without any shuffling of your feet into position, but with clean-cut precise movements.

You will find it advantageous to keep your knees slightly bent, and the arms hanging loosely at your sides.

We now come to the all important question of how to upset or unbalance the antagonist. By that is meant so to unbalance him that he is in danger of falling, and is, therefore, unable to control his strength.

There are *eight* directions in which this can be accomplished. He can be pushed backwards, pulled forwards, and moved to either side. But owing to the construction of the hip and knee joints he is enabled to recover his balance by simply stepping the same way in which his body is moving, and, consequently, he is not likely to be at all disturbed. *But when he is pulled or pushed diagonally*, a slight loss of balance occurs immediately, the reason being that his knee-joint is not hinged in the corner-ways direction, and his leg becomes stiff at once, and causes him to attempt to step across with his other foot in order to retain his upright posture.

This temporarily unbalanced position in an adversary is the one which you must always, in an encounter, try to bring about, and in all subsequent instructions, when you are told to " *break his posture*," the intention is that you shall " pull or push him to his left or right front or back *corner*."

A MOVE FOR A DESPERATE SITUATION— THE CROSS SWING AND CUT

For the first exploitation of this outstanding principle, let us suppose that you are gripped by the throat strongly with both hands. If you are securely held, no amount of violent struggling will get you free, but, instead, will waste your strength and gradually weaken you. So instead of endeavouring frantically to release yourself, just step *backwards diagonally* with your left foot, instantly drawing the right foot after it about six inches, so as to preserve that fundamental stance. *At the same time,* bring up your *right arm* over and across your adversary's two hands and continue the movement until it reaches round your neck on the *left* side. This should bring your right shoulder underneath your chin, and the effect of this action will

be to brush away his hands from your throat and also to tilt his body forward to his right front corner, with his face presenting a wide open target to receive a vicious jab from your elbow. The fact of your stepping back diagonally brings his body forward in a corresponding direction, causing him to lose his balance temporarily (Fig. 1).

Fig. 1

You can make *doubly* sure of causing this effect by bringing up your *left* hand just as you make your step diagonally backwards and dropping it lightly but clingingly on to his " near " wrist, in this case, his *right* one. By holding his hand where it is, *i.e.*, against your neck, you can make sure that his body is brought forward.

Now let us see if you have got it clearly. He grips your throat with both hands and you instantly :

Summary:

(1) Step back with your *left* foot.

(2) Draw the right after it quickly to assume the natural stance.

(3) Bring your right arm over and across his hands and swing to your *left*.

(4) Your *left* hand has meanwhile taken a hold on the nearest point, *i.e.*, his right wrist, and therefore assisted in pulling him off his balance.

A DEVASTATING BLOW

Fig. 2

You are now perfectly placed to deal him a damaging blow with your elbow, or, if his face is too far away, to strike him at the side of his neck with the little finger edge of your hand, *held rigidly*, and the arm bent at the elbow to form a right-angle.

You see that in this way you have a striking weapon some eighteen inches in length, an arm and hand that is swept round like a *scythe* (Fig. 2). A gentle trial will demonstrate that either the elbow or edge of your hand is *bound* to catch an antagonist, and you will readily agree, I think, that this blow is not only more effective, but is much easier and safer to land, than a blow with your fist, which invariably hurts your knuckles almost as much as it hurts your opponent.

This whole movement can be practised without an opponent, and it is not at all necessary to practise with both hands, but only with your favourite hand, which is usually your right. If you are *left*-handed, then step back with your *right* foot and bring your left arm across as explained.

The great value in this " cross swing and cut " lies in its general usefulness.

The " Cross Swing and Cut " will get you out of any " rough house."

IF HE GRABS BOTH YOUR COAT LAPELS: Step back as before, bringing your *right* arm across, and dropping your *left* hand on either his " near " wrist or sleeve (the nearest to your left hand in any case), and bring your elbow smashing into his face as he is jerked forward by your backward action (as Fig. 1).

IF HE TAKES A HOLD ON YOUR COLLAR with one hand whilst threatening you with a stick with the other : your defence is exactly the same—the cross swing and cut.

IF HE GRABS YOU BY BOTH ARMS AT THE ELBOWS: Proceed as before except that you will be unable to use your left hand for pulling him.

But the fact that he is bound to lean forward in order to hold you in this fashion will make amends for that.

IF HE GRIPS BOTH YOUR WRISTS: The same move applies, but this time bring your *right* arm inside (*i.e.*, against the gap formed by his thumb and forefinger) and strike as before.

IF YOU ARE MIXED UP IN A GENERAL SCUFFLE: Grab hold of the part of your adversary that is *nearest* to you, with your left hand, step back *diagonally* with your left foot and bring your *right* arm across and strike in the manner described, either at his face or body according to his position as you execute your unbalancing pull (Fig. 3).

BE CAREFUL WHEN PRACTISING

Realise, then, that you have now a most effective defence that can be utilised in almost any circumstances when the encounter is rough and dangerous. But be careful, when practising with a friendly partner, not actually to strike him in the face with your elbow or the edge of your hand. Stop the blow just before it lands : that will teach you to control your movements.

Fig. 3

CHAPTER II

TAKING PRISONER

When faced by a threatening enemy your first thought should be to put yourself in a position of comparative safety, that is, to hold him in such a way that he can do you no harm whilst you gain time to think what you are going to do with him.

Your safest place is obviously *behind him;* and you can accomplish this easily with the following move, which will also enable you to take him prisoner with little trouble and practically no risk to yourself.

Fig. 4

Step *diagonally* forwards with your *right* foot, bringing up the *left* after it to preserve your balance, and turn slightly *towards* him as you do so. Simultaneously your *right* hand takes a hold on his left sleeve just above the elbow and swings him round to his right, *i.e.,* away from you (Fig. 4).

Your left hand takes hold of his right upper arm holding it against his body, the push on his elbow being maintained with your right hand (Fig. 5).

This latter move will be greatly facilitated if you turn *well* towards him, *i.e.,* your chest being adjacent to his left shoulder.

Your next endeavour is to bring your buttocks behind him, and you will find this rather difficult if his body is held at all rigidly.

To overcome this trouble, then, move your right hand from his elbow, and, holding your fist *half* shut, dig your knuckles into his kidney (the soft part), and push sharply forwards and diagonally downwards.

Fig. 5

Fig. 6

Fig. 7

Properly applied this push is irresistible and the effect will be to cause his knees to bend and his back to hollow (Fig. 6.)

You now have plenty of room in which to step across with your left foot, bending your knees, and letting your left arm slide round his throat (Fig. 7).

It only remains now for you to walk forward, and, as he is

resting entirely on his heels he is completely *without balance* and therefore *without resistance.*

Your hands need not be clasped together as shown in the diagram unless he becomes excessively violent—an unlikely event in this position—and the right hand accordingly remains free to open doors or clear a passage for yourself.

SUMMARY

This most effective manœuvre is composed of three movements :

(1) Step up with your right foot and turn towards him, your right hand having grasped his sleeve and swung his shoulder round.

(2) Dig your right fist (half-shut) into his kidney and push diagonally forwards and downwards.

(3) Withdrawn your right fist and step across his back with your left foot, bending your knees, and bring your buttocks well across.

SOME CAPITAL MOVES FROM THE SAME PRINCIPLE

There are other methods of proceeding after you have " turned " him as in the first movement. Instead of throwing your left arm across his throat you can take hold of his *left* wrist as it is swung forward by the action of your right-hand grip.

As your left hand takes hold of his left wrist you step forward with your left foot and pull him forward slightly further to unbalance him, and then you *thrust* it (his left wrist) between his legs, where it is received by your *right* hand, which has meanwhile been taken from his sleeve and been brought behind him into position (Fig. 8).

Fig. 8

It is advisable to keep your chest close against his back as you execute this movement, the reason being that if you fumble and lose the grip on his left wrist it is an easy matter to regain control of him by slipping both your hands down his "near" leg and pulling his ankle backwards, and, at the same time, "bunting" his body forwards with your shoulder. This movement would bring him on to his face.

Now this move is most effective and quite simple and safe to execute, providing always that you perform the initial turning movement properly and rapidly.

It is only by continual practice that you can acquire this skill. Do it slowly at first, obtaining smoothness and grace until you can "turn" a man from almost any angle, and by simply hooking your hand round his upper arm.

ESCAPE FROM A NECK-HOLD

If your opponent swings his arm around your neck whilst facing you, it is still best to "turn" him, and you can do this by bringing up your right hand beneath his elbow (the thumb side towards you) and push upwards and slightly outwards. If you lower your body at the same time by bending your knees, his arm will come right over your head, when a little more push will turn him away from you, the back of his left shoulder coming in line with your chest (Fig. 9).

Your right hand should now be slid down to the hollow of his back (top of his buttocks is rather more precise) and a vigorous push diagonally forwards and downwards will bring about his very sudden downfall (Fig. 10).

There are numerous opportunities of adapting this principle in a scuffle, and it should be practised from both sides.

Fig. 9   Fig. 10

CHAPTER III

THE VULNERABLE WRIST

The movement of the wrist appears at first examination to be of a rotary nature, and when the fist is firmly clenched the wrist certainly has considerable strength and rigidity. But here again, that *cornerways* or *diagonal* direction manifests the weakness of this joint.

Get a friend to hold out, say, his left arm, take his hand in both yours, placing your thumbs on the back and your fingers in the palm. *Press your thumbs away from you and draw your fingers towards you* which will cause his hand to be bent towards *him*. He will experience no discomfort whatever from this, because his elbow will have bent also, and, consequently, neutralised your pressure.

Now repeat this movement, but this time bend his hand *diagonally backwards, i.e.,* towards his *left back corner*, your thumbs and fingers pressing in opposite directions as before. Do this very slowly and gently and warn him to *tap* on his leg or body with his right hand as soon as the pain is more than he can bear (inset to Fig. 11).

That then, briefly, is the principle of the wrist lock—to bend his wrist the *way it will not go*.

" But," your partner will say, " I could have resisted that lock quite easily."

Your partner is right—there is something lacking. Have you guessed what it is? Quite correct. He has not yet had his *balance* disturbed.

Now you have the whole idea roughly, and so let him be the attacker again and see how easily you can perform this most amazingly effective move.

Presume then, that he grabs you by the coat lapels, with his *left* hand, brandishing his *right* fist at you in a threatening manner. This action brings him forward on to his left toes.

As you start to step back, but not before, bring up your *right* hand, *over* his left, your fingers reaching round his thumb and embedding themselves firmly in his palm. Your thumb is pressed into the back of his hand, the tip of it being placed approximately an inch below the large knuckle of the third finger.

Your hand is now turned to the right and your *left hand* is brought up as a reinforcement, the thumb being placed *on top* of your right thumb and the fingers over your right fingers in his palm.

If you have a small hand, place the left thumb at the *side* of your right.

The pressure on his wrist can now be applied. He has lost his power of resistance, owing to the fact that he is in a " broken posture," which also explains why he cannot use his free (right) hand to hit you. So press your thumbs to his *left back corner*, and draw your fingers in precisely the opposite direction (Fig. 11).

Fig. 11

At the same time you should be careful to *keep your elbows fairly close* to your sides, and draw your hands towards your body as you press with your thumbs.

Thus you will have power over his hand and can either force him to the ground by continuing the outward twist, or make him howl for mercy by applying the pressure severely every time he attempts to move.

It is important to learn the "Outer Hand Twist" properly, as it is certainly one of the most attractive and easily applied moves in the range of antagonistics.

You can take an adversary's hand from any angle, whether he is grabbing you or not, and with constant practice you should be able to get it single handed (without needing your other hand for reinforcement) on a much bigger and stronger fellow than yourself. If it fails at all, you will probably :—

(1) Not have stepped back far enough to unbalance him ;

(2) Have placed your thumbs too high on the back of his hand ;

(3) Not got proper " contrary " movement in your thumbs and fingers ;

(4) Have your arms too straight and your elbows too far from your sides.

So practice, practice, practice until you can " find the right spot " in the dark.

AN ATTACKING WRIST THROW

Another wrist lock which is much simpler to learn than the foregoing, and is certain to bring down the toughest and most formidable opponent is the " Spinning Wrist Throw."

Suppose you and he are having a *scuffle at close quarters* and you want to finish him quickly, try this :

Slide your hands from his chest or shoulders down his left arm until you come to his hand. (This is always the best method of taking an antagonist's hand or arm, and it is much safer than grabbing at it.)

Your left fingers wrap round his thumb, holding it firmly whilst your *right* hand takes a natural but firm hold on his wrist.

You step back with your *left* foot with a *turning motion* to

your left, and carry his hand over your head, continuing your *turn* by bringing your *right* foot up until you are facing him again (Fig. 12). This action, as you will realise, will have twisted his wrist in an outward direction, and if you proceed with the twist, he is

Fig. 12

bound to fall heavily on his back.

The important points in this move are :—

(1) To step back so quickly that he is practically jerked forward ;

(2) To make your turn very rapidly, and to make sure to be *moving away from him* whilst doing it, for otherwise *his arm will bend*, and you will lose the effect ;

(3) To hold his wrist and hand firmly throughout and *not* to let your hands cross at the completion of your turn.

(4) To always turn *outside* his arm.

As for the " outer hand twist," it is essential that practice be constant until grace and speed are achieved.

CHAPTER IV

THE PRINCIPLE OF THE STRAIGHT ARM LOCK

In making personal contact with an enemy, who may resort to any means to put you off your guard, the need for actually disabling him is manifest.

Here then are a series of locks by which you can either inflict severe pain upon him or completely dislocate one or both elbow joints.

The elbow is a hinged joint, and therefore has a limited movement. That limit is reached when the arm is fully extended. Any further pressure in that direction, any attempt to force it to go beyond the limit, would cause instant and excruciating pain, as the tendons and ligaments that join the biceps to the muscles of the forearm become strained ; and, if the pressure were proceeded with, they would become considerably torn, and dislocation of the joint would take place.

This latter event is invariably avoided in friendly combat. A partner-opponent would be crying aloud for relief long before this happened. And, in the practice of these extremely dangerous locks your partner-antagonist must be told, in order to prevent the breaking of his limbs, to tap with his hand on your body as soon as pain is felt, as a signal that you have gone far enough.

The first thing to learn, then, is to appreciate the principle by which the arm of your adversary can be forced slightly beyond its natural limit.

This is achieved by the simple mechanical principle of lever and fulcrum.

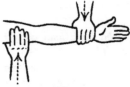

Fig. 13

The fulcrum must always be placed under the upper arm just above the elbow, and the leverage is obtained by the pressure of your hands on your adversary's wrist (Fig. 13).

It is also necessary to prevent his shoulder from moving and thus minimising the pain, and this is done by various means according to the method of applying the lock.

Here is a way of demonstrating the principle, with dire results to the victim.

Suppose you have brought him to the ground with the " Spinning Wrist Throw " described in Lesson 3, and he tries to avoid further consequence by squirming his body away from you.

Fig. 14

You still have a grip on his hand, so raise your " near " foot (in this case your *right*) and place it on his chest and under his armpit, remembering to " snuggle " your little toe edge as close as possible.

Your *right* knee comes *outside* his arm, your shinbone thus forming the fulcrum just above his elbow, and by pulling your hands towards yourself and pushing your knee slightly forward, you can obtain great leverage against his elbow joint. Your foot on his chest keeps his shoulder from moving and his arm is securely " locked." Pressure should now be applied very slowly, and here an important factor must be observed.

That is, that the *little finger edge of his hand must always be kept " in line " with the fulcrum* you apply (see Fig. 13).

This will be made abundantly clear in future descriptions of straight arm locks; but try to get the idea at once, for it will save you much futile effort.

So that in this " Foot on chest " arm lock, his little finger should be nearest to you and his thumb furthest away.

HERE IS A " COME-ALONG " ARM LOCK that will further help you to appreciate the principle, and is useful in taking a prisoner.

Take hold of his left wrist (as described in Lesson 3) by sliding your hands to it, and spring back with your left foot, turning somewhat to your left as you do so. This

Fig. 15

disturbs his posture, and as his arm becomes extended, throw your *right arm over his upper arm*, your right hand eventually taking a hold on your own coat lapel.

You now turn his hand so that his little finger edge is bottom-most, and a gentle pressure downwards will cause him such agony as to make resistance impossible.

THE GOLF-SWING ARM-LOCK

Another easily applied arm-lock can be obtained if you happen to take hold of his left wrist with your left hand, your fingers being uppermost.

Step back as before with your left foot, turning *half left* as you do so.

Your *right* hand is now brought on to his wrist, your fingers also being uppermost, *i.e.*, your thumbs being adjacent to each other.

Obviously, he has been pulled forward in a diagonal direction, as you stepped back, and that pull is now continued, with the help of your two hands, in a *downward* curve, rather in the manner of a golf swing, your arms being practically straight.

This will cause him to bend forward with all his weight on the little toe corner of his foot, and with his arm fully extended. Your *right forearm* is now pressed along and across his, your elbow bearing on his upper arm, just above the elbow.

Fig. 16

Your *left hand* continues the curving pull in an upward direction, the little finger edge of his hand being *nearest* to you and therefore in direct line with the fulcrum that you supply with your right elbow.

Your antagonist will probably fall on his face to try and ease the pain at his elbow joint, and, if this happens, just substitute your right *hand* for your elbow, straightening your right arm, and you can keep him down suffering excruciating pain as long as you wish.

SECRET OF SUCCESS

The secret of success in achieving any of these locks is, however, found in the first move you make in the preliminary pull and step backwards to disturb his balance. I think you will realise by this time that so called "tricks" of self-defence matter very little indeed unless the principle is applied.

The beginning and end of all knowledge of how to overcome an antagonist, be he stronger or weaker than yourself, is "balance"—the building up of your own mental and physical balance. To the question, "What should you do if you were attacked in a certain manner?" the reply is "It all depends on his movement." It also all depends on your state of mind at the moment. Therefore the best advice I can offer you during your study of "Unarmed Combat" is to learn these moves for the development of confidence in yourself, and to try always to see how the principles expounded can be applied to enable you to take advantage of an adversary's movement. Don't try to catalogue your knowledge in a list of numerous so called "tricks," but extend that knowledge on your own account by developing your ability to utilise his every movement to his own disadvantage. Realise that his impetus must never be interrupted, but only misdirected. When he aims a blow at you and you stop that blow with your arm, don't continue to resist his force, but turn your body so that his viciousness is carried on, not at you, but past you.

For example, when a much bigger and stronger opponent comes at you viciously, do not under any circumstances try to parry the attack with arm locks or wrist locks, but just grab his clothing at his chest, and throw him with this amazingly simple, yet most effective and (to the recipient) terrifying, "stomach throw."

As you grab his clothing with both hands step in between his feet, with, say, your *left* foot. Bend the knee well forward and sit down on the ground close to your *left* heel, at the same time raising your right foot and placing it against his body at the groin. Keep your arms fairly straight as you roll on your back up to your shoulders.

Fig. 17

Do not push with your foot against his body until he has passed the point of balance and is falling, but a little lift at this moment will bring him over your head, and he will make a most unhappy landing on the back of his neck.

This and the *ankle roll* explained in Chapter VI are far and away the most simple and certain ways of bringing down a powerful adversary providing you have room in which to throw him.

CHAPTER V

THE ART OF " BREAKING YOUR FALL " WHEN THROWN

An excellent method of increasing the blood circulation and toning up the muscles.

In subsequent chapters will be described various developments of the already defined methods of disturbing an opponent's balance, and you will be shown how, with little effort, you can throw him to the ground with sufficient force to finish the combat at once.

But much practice is needed to acquire this skill, and you must have a sensible friend upon whom to try these throws.

Your first question will be : " Ah, but what about him ? Will he not get rather badly knocked about ? Or perhaps break his collar-bone ? "

The answer to that is : " No, he will not. In fact, he will thoroughly enjoy being thrown : and so will you as soon as you have got a rough idea of the Japanese art of ' break-falling '."

The first few minutes of indulgence in this lesson will also show you that you have found one of the most exhilarating of all the varied phases of physical culture.

A " break-fall " is accomplished by striking the ground with all your available " muscle-pads," at the same time distributing the shock of the fall over as large an area (of ground) as possible. The reason for this will be quite clear to you when you recall that your natural instinct, when falling, is to stretch out your hand to save yourself, so leaving your wrist (a very weak member) to receive the whole weight of the falling body, which in all probability results in a sprain or fracture.

The Japanese exponent of Judo (or Ju-Jitsu), when he is thrown, strikes the ground with his hand and arm, *palm downwards*, the blow being made with the " muscle-pads " from the fingers, soft part of the forearm, and upper arm right up to the large pads behind the shoulders, the arm acting like a spring and the percussion absorbing the shock.

The blow delivered must register a greater pressure than the weight of the falling body, and must strike the ground at the same instant as the body ; and, therefore, the timing of the blow is most important.

Your initial practice, then, is concerned chiefly with learning to " beat " or strike the ground properly and it is best if you can obtain a couple of old mattresses, or two thick carpets, or anything else to minimise the hardness of the floor.

BEATING THE BLOW

First of all then :

Lie flat on your back, drawing up your feet and raising your hips so that only your feet and shoulders are touching the floor, your chin being kept on your chest and your head never being allowed to fall back. Bring your right arm across your body, bending the elbow easily until your right hand touches your left shoulder. Now swing back sharply, hitting the mat about a foot from your body, and letting your right hip come down with it to add force to the blow. Your fingers will probably tingle at first, but the immediate improvement in your blood circulation will more than compensate for that.

Return your arm across your body, swinging easily on to the left shoulder pad, and repeat the blow, striking a bit harder this time. Now, as the right arm makes the blow bring your left arm across to your right shoulder and perform the same movement on that side ; then, alternately, so that as one arm " beats the mats " the other comes to the " across body " position. Continue this exercise for about a dozen times, increasing the force of the blow each time, and then get up and see how you feel. Your whole body will be tingling and glowing as though you have just finished a sharp walk, and your brain will become alert as the blood is enlivened from the effects of the percussion. Not only have you achieved the object of all physical culture, which is the improving of the blood circulation, but you have also got the rudiments of breaking your fall (Fig. 18). (Right leg is shown extended for clearness.)

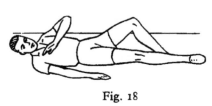

Fig. 18

LEARNING TO TIME THE BLOW

The next thing to learn is the timing of the blow. This can be accomplished very simply. Sit up, one knee being drawn in close to your chin, the other leg extended straight out in front of you. Hold your right arm above your head, the left hand being placed on the ground palm downwards, ready to assist the next movement. Roll back, keeping your legs in the same position—*i.e.*, bringing them with you—and, as your shoulders touch the ground, bring the right arm down and beat hard as in the last exercise. Come back to sitting position and repeat until your blow is so crisp and properly timed that it almost shoots your legs over your head. When you have got to this stage, it is time to start to fall, so return to the sitting position and raise yourself about two or three

inches from the ground with the aid of the left hand. Roll
back and beat hard, but this time turn your head to the right
and keep your chin on your chest so that your head will not
strike the ground. Return to sitting position each time with
an easy swing, and gaining momentum by pushing your
chin forward over your left knee, and by lifting more with
your left hand, gradually fall from a greater height, until
you can land without any shock to your body from a height of
about twelve or fifteen inches. The chief points to remember
are to strike hard, to fall on the " shoulder-pad " (or latissimus
dorsi muscle) and to turn your head towards the striking arm.
By this time you will have developed a certain amount of
confidence, and this can be quickly increased by another
exercise.

Fig. 19

Get your friend with
whom you are practising
to stand firm by your left
side as you lie on the
ground.   With   your
left hand take hold of both
his coat lapels or his
bent forearm, and raise
your body to a height of
about a foot from the
floor.   Then fall in the
manner already described,
hitting the ground harder

each time according to the height to which you raise yourself
(Fig. 19). When you can do this without receiving any
shock to your body, you will be able to take any throw
given to you on that side without any discomfort whatever, and it therefore remains to commence the last two
exercises all over again, transposing the striking arm to the
left.

The most fascinating exercise in the whole series of Breakfall movements is the " Forward Rolling Breakfall."

The object of this is to avoid any shock to the body when you are thrown " heels over head," such as you would be if you were thrown from a horse or cycle. " Falling " throws taught to you in later lessons also necessitate the use of this particular fall to avoid shock.

The idea is to turn your body into a wheel and so prevent any point from receiving the full brunt of the weight.

Start to practice this way :

Place your *left* foot forward.   Now bend down and put your *right* hand on the ground in front of your *left* foot.

The next move is most important :

Swing your *left* arm up and behind you continuing the swing forward, in front of and over your head with your hand turned *palm* inwards (Fig. 20).

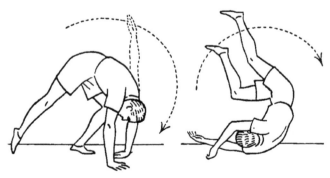

Fig. 20   Fig. 21

Holding your left arm fairly rigid although slightly bent, pitch your body forward in a rolling action led by your left arm (Fig. 21). The back of your left shoulder will then touch the ground, and, as the roll is continued, you will turn completely over, coming up on your right side.

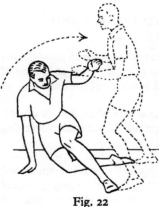

Fig. 22

After some practice you should cross your legs as they come over, which will have the effect of bringing you upright facing the way you started, and completely " in balance." (See dotted lines, Fig. 22.)

CHAPTER VI

A NOVEL WAY TO DISARM AND
DISABLE HIM

When you are attacked by a man who is considerably heavier and stronger than yourself, my original advice to " First of all disturb his balance " may fill you with a little misgiving.

Presume he is much bigger than you, then, and he squares up to you looking really dangerous, his attitude suggesting that he is about to hit you.

Your first anxiety is to place yourself in a safe position, and the first " turning movement " given in Lesson 2 should carry you close to him and reasonably safe for the moment.

Fig. 23

Now, bring your *left* foot between his and turned in somewhat (pigeon-toed), bending your knee, and, at the same time, slightly swinging round to your right.

This will enable you to roll to the ground on your *right* side, placing, as you do so, your *right* foot against the front of his *left* shin bone (Fig. 23).

Your hands have, in the meantime, taken a hold on his *left* sleeve and *right* armpit respectively, and will enable you to pull him over your right side as you fall back, which

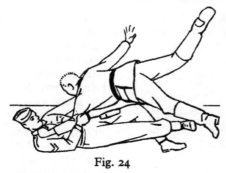

will cause him to land on his back with great force (Fig. 24).

This throw we will call "ankle roll" and is fairly simple to bring off even on the toughest of opponents, and practice will

Fig. 24

enable you to execute it with lightning rapidity.

You should take great care to fall on your *right side—NOT* on your back, as by doing this you will probably bring his chest crashing down on to your own face.

Your *right* foot should perform a slight lifting action as he is falling and this will ensure him landing on his shoulder. That will probably shake him up so severely that the encounter will end abruptly.

In any case it is wise to make doubly sure, and I am now going to describe a method of holding him down, so that no matter how he struggles he will not be able to escape.

This is accomplished by the scientific distribution of your body weight, and it can be used to follow immediately the foregoing throw.

So we will revert to the presumption that you have just brought him down with "Ankle roll" and he has landed on his back about a yard away from your right side.

It is important that you should have retained your *right* hand grip on his left sleeve, but you should, of course, loose your left hand grip, as he is falling.

Now, quickly turn your body towards him, rolling right over on to your chest, at the same time reaching for his neck

 with your left arm. Continue your rolling movement, bringing your *left leg underneath* you (Fig. 25), finally drawing yourself up to his side in a half-sitting posture as in the accompanying sketch.

Fig. 25

Your *right hand* preserves its grip on his sleeve which you now hug tightly to your body with a firm pull.

Your *left* arm has gone round his neck—it should *not* however, grip too tightly, and your elbow and forearm must remain on the ground. This forms a sort of strut, for the right side of his body, and your legs form struts for the other side. Your left leg should be bent at a right-angle and your right leg placed well back.

If you now *relax* your muscles completely, you will find that no matter how he struggles he cannot possibly effect an escape.

It is important to keep your head well down, pressing it against the side of his. This not only helps to keep him down, but also prevents him from frantically clawing at your face.

If, when you practice this " hold-down," your friend manages to escape, then you are either :—

    (1) Tightening your muscles and therefore making yourself easy to move ; or,

(2) Not placing your " struts " correctly, as shown.

After thirty seconds or so of vain struggling your " victim " will be exhausted and you can apply this powerful arm-lock :

Abandon your hold on his sleeve and take hold of his wrist and push it underneath your left leg as shown by the dotted lines in the sketch (Fig. 25).

Your left leg is brought down to " clip " it firmly in place of your hand, and, instantly, considerable pain is caused to his elbow joint.

You now have him completely at your mercy, and you can increase the pain by placing your right hand under his elbow and lifting it up, or pressing down on his elbow with your right hand and raising your hips from the ground.

I know you will appreciate that this " *side sitting hold down* " can be used from any position during a scuffle on the ground, and practice will enable you to drop comfortably into it on either side of your assailant's body no matter how he tries to squirm away from you.

There is just a chance, however, that if you slightly relax your hold on his left sleeve, he may manage to wriggle his elbow in such a way as to get his left hand underneath your chin, and, by pushing your head upwards, so weaken your position as to be able to pull you over his body.

Here is where you are enabled to utilize the principle of non-resistance. Resist his pressure ever so slightly in order to make him push harder and then suddenly bring your *right* hand against the outside of his elbow and push inwards (to your left) so that his arm is slid *past* your head, so to speak. Your head can now be lowered again alongside his head, the difference being that his shoulder and upper arm are being pressed against the side of his neck. Your right

Fig. 26

hand now slips under his neck, and joins your own left hand, gripping it round the little finger edge, which brings the sharp edge of your wrist (the thumb side) pressing against the far side of his neck at the carotid artery (Fig. 26).

So, by boring the side of your head against his, and pulling towards you with your hands, you can cause him really severe pain since his upper arm is practically choking him. Submission, in the circumstances, will be speedily forthcoming.

Again, if he succeeds in keeping his arm close to his side, so that you are unable to draw his sleeve round your waist, there occurs an opportunity to apply a really paralysing " nerve pressure." You will, of course, be unable to employ either of the foregoing locks, but you must keep your head alongside his all the same, " boring " at his temple with the side and back of your head.

There is a spot on the neck just below the ear which is extremely sensitive to a sharp pressure—you will find the exact place by experiment—and if you bore into this with the second or large knuckle of the second finger of your right hand, holding the fist half shut, you will be surprised at the alacrity with which he yells " Kamerad."

The important thing is to draw his head towards you with your left arm, which encircles his neck, and at the same time to press the opposite way with your head. The rest is simple and speedy.

CHAPTER VII

TURNING THE TABLES WHEN YOU ARE KNOCKED DOWN

Now, here is a new angle on the subject—the reply to a question which I have no doubt has already occurred to you. " What about if *he* lands the first blow ? "

Well, I can assure you, if he hits you hard on the point of the jaw, you will probably be in a bad way, and it depends on your toughness and " guts " whether you will be able to carry on or not.

But, with the agility and alertness you should have acquired by practice of the movements involved during practice in Unarmed Combat you should be able to avoid that happening.

Let us presume that in a promiscuous " scrap " he has been able to knock you down and promptly bends over you, grabbing you by the throat with the obvious intention of " finishing you off."

You are lying flat on your back, and he approaches from your *right* side both his hands gripping your throat, his *right* arm being naturally the "near" arm (that is, nearest to *you*.).

Although it now seems that you haven't a chance, you can easily and with one rapid movement " turn the tables."

Bring your *left* hand on top of his right wrist, and, bending your *right* leg, draw the lower part of it (*i.e.*, the shin-bone) underneath his right armpit. This movement is made much easier if you pull hard on his right arm.

At the same time, raise your *left* leg, taking it over his head and in front of his face until your calf is brought against his throat.

It is most important to keep your right leg well bent, the muscles being held very loosely, so that your heel almost presses into your thigh or buttock.

Fig. 27

If you now straighten up your body, you will be applying a very powerful *straight arm lock*, the fulcrum being formed by your crutch, which comes just above his elbow, and you can obtain terrific leverage by " hollowing " your back somewhat and raising your hips.

What will probably happen, however, is that when you bring your *left* leg over his head with a swing, he will be rolled over on to his back, still, of course, with his arm firmly held between your thighs, and suffering extreme pain at the elbow joint.

Now this " *straight arm-lock between thighs* " is the perfect example of the principle of lever and fulcrum expounded to you in Chapter 4. Once this lock is successfully applied *there is no escape from it* whatever, no matter how powerful or experienced your adversary may be.

In the case of an enemy you could be utterly ruthless and break the arm.

It can be applied from many angles, whether you are on top, or underneath, the successful execution of it depending entirely on your suppleness and easy movement.

Exponents of the Japanese art of Judo or Ju-Jitsu exploit it considerably, even deliberately allowing an opponent to get on top of them in order to secure it, and thus demonstrating the outstanding precept of this art, viz., " winning by appearing to lose."

Here is a way of applying this lock after you have managed to throw your assailant with say " The Spinning Wrist Throw " or the " Outer Hand Twist " : You have brought

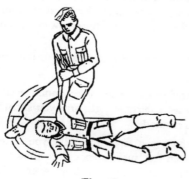

him down and are standing at his left side, still holding his left hand or wrist. Advance your left leg, until the foot is underneath his shoulder and the shinbone is pressing against his armpit. Now push your knee forward so that you are practically kneeling on his body.

Fig. 28

Suddenly sit down, your buttock coming as close as possible to your left heel, and, at the same time, swing your right leg over and across his face (Fig. 28) until you are lying at

right-angles to him, your left knee being upright and his arm firmly held between your thighs (Fig. 29).

You can now apply the lock by raising your hips slightly as you pull down on his arm .

Fig. 29

I think you will realise from the description given that the method of application is similar whether the lock be applied from " on top " or " underneath."

The chief points to observe in the performance of these movements are :—

(1) Your adversary's arm must be *pulled* towards you the whole time.

(2) You must make sure of being close to him ; which means that if you sit too far away the fulcrum (your crutch) will be on the wrong side of the elbow joint, and the lock will fail.

(3) Your thighs must squeeze this arm tightly, so that he cannot wriggle.

So that, if you are engaged in a struggle on the ground, every time your opponent exposes a fairly straight arm you should be able to lock it, by this method.

When he attempts to push you away from him, you resist his push, but *only so far*—in fact, just far enough to allow his arm to become straight—and then . . . drop your shin against his body, swing your other leg round and sit down, rolling on your back as you do so . . . and the combat is finished, as the pain will compel him instantly to submit.

Let me conclude this lesson with a very valuable tip.

Just as your first endeavour in an upstanding encounter should be to disturb his balance, so should your first object in groundwork be to *get your legs around his body*.

By that I mean, entwine your legs around his waist, and then it matters not at all whether you are " on top " or " underneath," you are definitely in the best position.

If, for example, you are lying on your back with your legs around his waist, and he attempts to strangle you or punch you, all you have to do is to swing, say, your left leg over his right arm, bringing it over his head and in front of his face, the calf of your leg eventually coming under his throat (as in Fig. 27—page 38).

With the aid of this limb you roll him over on to his back, and his arm can be locked as before, except that both his legs will now be across his body.

All you have to do now is to entwine your ankles and his arm can be firmly clipped between your thighs. Now raise your hips and pull his arm towards you (in the direction of the little finger-edge of his hand), and he can do nothing but " tap " the mat.

This lock can, of course, be operated from the other side and from many other angles when your man exposes a straight arm and you have your legs free.

So experiment with your partner slowly and carefully, avoiding all *jerking* when applying the lock, as this will endanger his elbow-joint.

CHAPTER VIII

WHEN YOU ARE CAUGHT UNAWARES

When an assailant, catching you in an unguarded moment and totally unprepared for an attack, manages to pin both your arms against your body, then you are most certainly in an awkward predicament.

In the first place you should never have been caught " off the alert " mentally or physically. By which I infer that you should cultivate the adoption of the " fundamental stance " at all times.

After keeping your mind on this for a week or so you will find that it is very much more comfortable to stand " balanced " (*i.e.*, with your body weight evenly distributed, your chin in, your arms hanging loosely at your sides and the knees straight but not flexed) than it is to stand in a lounging attitude, with your hands in your pockets, your chest sunken (thereby constricting abdominal function) and, in short, only half awake.

You will find that the adoption of correct stance, keeps you mentally alert and gives you a wonderful sense of well-being and supreme confidence.

But, supposing you *are* caught, then you must quickly effect an escape and take revenge without more ado.

To explain the method of achieving this result we will presume that he has thrown his arms round your body from the front, clasping his hands behind you and thus securing your arms completely.

If his legs are apart, use your knee viciously at his

Fig. 30

fork, to make him relax his grip. But if his feet are close together use the following nerve pressure.

Approximately two inches from either hip bone and on the " line of the groin " is situated the " femoral nerve."

Your thumbs are therefore brought against these nerves and a vigorous pressure exerted (Fig. 30).

The pain from this is so sharp that he will be bound to withdraw his body slightly, even though he does not release his grip, and this gives you an opportunity to execute an excellent and most devastating throw called " The Hip Throw."

The moment his body is drawn away from you, start to twist your buttocks round towards him by stepping up with your *right* foot, placing it between his feet. At the same time let your *right* arm slide either round his waist or behind

Fig. 31

his left shoulder, and *pivot* on your right foot so as to bring your buttocks against his abdomen with your *knees well bent* (Fig. 31).

Your left foot should be drawn up to assume the fundamental position and your left hand takes a hold on his *right sleeve* above the elbow.

Now, keeping your knees bent, push your *buttocks* back into his abdomen, at the same time pulling hard across your body with your *left* hand, and he will be thrown literally heels over head to land flat on his back on the ground.

Considerable practice is required to make the turn and throw with the easy grace essential to success, but once acquired it is a standard throw that can be used in any emergency, from either side, and will succeed during an encounter with a much stronger and heavier opponent.

In fact, the taller the antagonist is, the better for you, for as long as he is close enough to you, it does not matter what sort of grip he has, the *hip throw* being applicable under almost any circumstances.

A MOVE THE SENTRY MUST REMEMBER

Presume that you are on guard and are attacked from *behind*. Your adversary is gripping you over both arms. You are in a distinctly awkward predicament. So here is a capital move to enable you to " turn the tables " just as easily and effectively as you did from the front.

If the assailant's grip is strong and powerful I know you will have difficulty in moving your arms, so your first object is to give yourself room to turn your body.

Keeping your arms fairly rigid, *cross* them in front of your body, and turn your hands outwards (*i.e.*, the little finger of

Fig. 32

either hand is to the front). This movement is not at all difficult to do, and it has the effect of pushing away his arms slightly and enables you to *turn* to your *right* somewhat, bringing your *right* foot round the outside of his *left* and placing it on the ground *behind him.*

There is no need to move your *left* foot, but *bend* your knees deeply and bring your

hands across the *front* of his body, taking his *legs* behind
and just below the knees, and lift *forwards* and *upwards* with
a scooping action, your knees *remaining bent*. As you do this
your shoulder butts him in the chest and he is thrown
heavily backwards, your *right* thigh forming a pivot over
which his body revolves (Fig. 32).

A FINE ATTACKING THROW

This "scooping throw" is easily made both from this
position and from the front.

If your antagonist is standing facing you, merely threatening
you with violence, you can upset his calculations by stepping
in with a turning action, your right foot being swung round
the back of his *left*, and your arms reaching across the front
of his body, to take his knees and scoop forward and upward
as before (see Fig. 32).

I strongly advise you to practice this move until you can
perform it with lightning rapidity, for it is an excellent way
to tackle an armed opponent, inasmuch as it places you
reasonably safe from damage whilst you are attempting it.

Now in all probability, an assailant upon whom you
managed to bring off the "scooping throw" in the street,
would be instantly rendered "hors de combat" by the fall.
But in the event of his surviving this, you should be able to
punish him further in order to make him fully appreciate
that he cannot get away with it.

You can do this, I know, by means of the arm locks you
have already learnt, but following this throw his legs will be
nearest to you and present you with a golden opportunity of
further demonstrating your skill and power in a way that is
safe for you and severe for him. So, as soon as he is on his
back seize one of his legs, say, his *right* with your left hand
under the calf. Whip it up sharply to a position under-

Fig. 33

neath your *right* armpit. Your right arm is now thrown round his leg, the *sharp edge* of your forearm coming against the lower part of his calf. *Close* your right fist and place it in the palm of your left hand (Fig. 33).

Running vertically in the calf muscle is the *posterior tibial nerve*, and by bending your knees and bringing your hips forward and your shoulders back, you can press your right forearm into his calf and cause him unbearable pain. He can ease this pain slightly by raising his body, but if you lift your *right* leg between his and place your *right* foot on the ground at the right side of his body you can prevent any further movement on his part.

You can increase his punishment, and subdue him still further, by retaining your hold and *sitting down*, interlocking

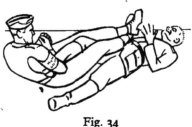

Fig. 34

your ankles as you do so, and, by raising your hips (which causes your forearm to press deeply into his legs) you can make him howl for mercy, especially if you use your heel viciously at his fork (Fig. 34).

This calf-muscle lock is dreadfully painful to the victim and is easily applied whenever you have thrown your man, or are grappling with him on the ground.

Fig. 35

Another application of this lock is open to you when your antagonist has you seemingly beaten by strangling you from behind, preventing you from wriggling by entwining his legs around your body (as Fig. 35). You would probably be able to struggle to a sitting position, from which you can turn the tables on the " strangler "

in a most effective and yet simple fashion.

If one presumes that your antagonist's *left* leg is crossed over his *right* leg, then you bring up your own *right* leg and place the calf on top of the toes of his *left* foot, hooking your

Fig. 36

leg over his foot, so to speak. Then, *raise your hips,* keeping your own right foot firmly on the ground (Fig. 36).

This action will cause his calf muscle (the posterior tibial nerve) to be pressed strongly against his own shin and he will not only be virtually locked himself, to the complete cessation

of any further aggressive action, but he will also be in such agonising pain that he will hasten to let go his stranglehold on you with extreme alacrity.

Should your antagonist's right leg be crossed over his left in his scissors grip on your body, then, of course, you bring up your left leg and hook over his right foot.

CHAPTER IX

NECK LOCKS

The neck is a particularly weak part of the human frame and
it is peculiarly susceptible to attack, the most vulnerable
points being the throat, the cavities on either side the
" Adam's Apple," and the *carotid* arteries (*i.e.*, those two
large veins that lie on either side the neck in a line from
above the shoulder to below the ear). As everybody knows,
the carotid arteries convey the blood from the heart to the
brain, and any stoppage of that function causes a slight
cerebral anaemia, and, if proceeded with, complete unconsciousness.

Now, if you have need to overpower a dangerous enemy it
is a simple matter for you to cause this stoppage.

Suppose you have thrown him by one of the methods already
taught, you should instantly drop on top of him, getting astride
him with your legs, your knees coming on to the ground near
to his armpits, your head lowered until it is pressing against
the side of his, and your forearms being placed either on the
ground under his upper arms or on the " crook " of each of
his arms. This is a complete hold down and he will be
unable to punch or do anything to you as you are too close.

Then insert your *right* thumb into the left side of his tunic
collar, the fingers coming outside, naturally.

Keep that grip and swing your body slightly to your *left*
so that your *right elbow* passes round the top of his head, the
forearm coming underneath.

Complete the circle and the little finger edge of your *right*
forearm will be bearing hard against the side of his neck,
across the *carotid artery*.

That will probably cause him to " gurgle " somewhat, but make sure of putting him out of action by inserting your *left* hand under your right and seizing the opposite lapel of his coat (his left) with your *palm* upwards.

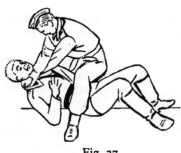

Fig. 37

You can now exert a scissor-like action against his neck, raising your left knee to get more leverage, and bearing down hard with your right forearm. Unconsciousness should supervene in about 12 to 15 seconds (Fig. 37).

The same principle applies to the "choke" or strangle shown in Fig. 38, but it is much better to obtain this *on the ground*, with your legs entwined round his body, than standing up, but the drawing is made from the latter position so that you can see the method of obtaining the hold and applying the lock more clearly.

Fig. 38

In this method you will observe that the pressure is directed against the " Adam's Apple " and prevents the victim breathing freely. Leverage is obtained by forcing your *left* elbow away from you and drawing his right coat lapel towards you.

If you apply this lock from a standing position it is best to place your *left* leg across the front of both his ; you can then keep him unbalanced by drawing him slightly forward on to his toes.

A QUICK ONE

Here is a very rapid method of demoralising the enemy.

Simply take his tunic collar in either hand, close to his neck.

Fig. 39

Your fingers take the underneath grip and your thumbs are pushed hard into his throat on either side the "A d a m ' s Apple." Your fingers make an upward lift on the coat to obtain greater leverage (Fig. 39).

Great care should be taken when practising this " choke," as injury may result from an over-enthusiastic application to your " friendly " victim.

A SURPRISING ATTACK

One of the most easily obtained neck locks, however, is what is known as the " Front Chancery." At first sight it may appear difficult to get a man's head under your arm, but if you follow the instructions carefully you will be surprised how many really " tough " opponents " fall for it."

A threat of violence is invariably accompanied by a thrusting forward of the chin, and that movement is your " cue " for action.

Swing your *right* arm forward, keeping it fairly rigid and bring the palm of your hand against the back of his neck.

The weight of your body can be added to the swing by bringing your shoulder forward, and, continuing round to your *left*, cause his head to come forward and downward to a position underneath your *left* arm, the arm being lifted to receive it.

The edge of the forearm (thumb-side) is now brought

across his throat and your right hand takes a grip on your left as reinforcement (Fig. 40).

To drive the forearm deeply into his throat all that you need do is to push your hips forward and your shoulders well back, lifting upwards as you do so. You can now use your foot or knee against his fork should circumstances demand it.

Fig. 40

This " Front Chancery " can be employed under any circumstances when his head happens to be lowered as, for instance, when he makes a grab for your legs (as for a Rugby tackle) or when he is rising from the floor after you have thrown him.

STALKING A SENTRY

You are already aware of the advantages of " turning " your adversary. His resistance is obviously much less when his *back* is towards you.

For example, if you are ever allotted the job of removing a sentry from his post it will have to be done with a complete absence of noise and with the utmost speed and certainty.

So, if you have made your approach stealthily it needs
very little effort to spring on to his back, knocking away his
rifle, of course, as you do so. You then bring your left hand
round to his mouth, your right hand being thrust against the
small of his back in a manner similar to the move shown in
Chapter II. If you now step back, jabbing your right foot
at the back of his knee to make sure, and draw him diagonally
downwards—that is towards you, of course—he will be
brought sharply to a sitting posture, when you can apply
the following effective " back-strangle."

As soon as you are behind him, slip your left arm round his
neck, the edge of the forearm (thumb side) coming across his

throat. With this hand you can
take a hold on his right coat lapel,
and all that remains is to push
his head forward with your right
hand, pulling hard with your left
and obtaining leverage from the
coat.

This hold can be made much
more severe and punishing if you
slip your right arm underneath
his right arm, and then bring it
round to the back of his head.
This, in addition to the
" strangle " causes a terrific
strain on his right shoulder, and
you will find him " tapping " the
instant it is applied (Fig. 41).

Fig. 41

CHAPTER X

THE " TRUSSED ARM " LOCK PRINCIPLE

The weakest part of the arm is the elbow, and when that elbow is moved like a " *crank* " (circularly outwards and upwards) it has practically no resistance.

Suppose, for instance, you antagonist takes a double-handed grip on your throat, his arms being bent slightly.

Place your right hand *underneath* his left elbow, the thumb being inside and the fingers out ; your left hand comes *on top* of his *right* elbow, the fingers being uppermost. Now make a sort of see-saw movement pushing upwards and to your left with your right hand and downwards and inwards with your left.

Your victim will be quite unable to resist this movement, especially if your hips are brought somewhat forward to support your arms. If you now turn your back to him, your buttocks coming against his loins you will arrive at a position similar to that depicted on Fig. 31, except that both his arms will be in your grip and he will be quite unable to save himself when you give him the " hip throw."

The point which I wish to emphasise, however, is the ease with which you can manipulate his arms when they are moved *circularly* at the elbow, or, to be more precise, in " crank-fashion."

So when you wish to weaken an otherwise strong arm, move the elbow outwards or inwards in an upward or downward curve.

Here is a splendid example of this precept and a lock that is of general utility.

AN ATTACKING LOCK

Your opponent is standing facing you with his arms in a natural sort of position, *i.e.*, hanging at his sides.

Bring up your left arm across his body, your hand being inserted *inside* and round the back of his left elbow, *i.e.*, between his arm and body.

Simultaneously, you must step diagonally (forward and outwards) with your right foot, a very similar move to the turning principle explained in Chapter II, except that you use the opposite hand.

This is important, as, extending your left arm across his body would leave you open and unbalanced, if you did it without moving your foot.

Your left hand now draws his elbow *outwards* and *towards* you, at the same time the *back* of your right hand being placed against his wrist and pushing him in the opposite direction. This has the effect of twisting his body, his fore-arm coming behind his back.

Fig. 42

Your right hand is now slid under his forearm, until it takes a hold (fingers on top) of his *upper* arm (Fig. 42).

If your right shoulder is now brought downwards to " clip " his arm your *left* can be taken away, but you can make sure by placing the thumb on top of his elbow as in the sketch.

The right foot should be brought forward to maintain your " fundamental " stance.

This particular exploitation

of the crank principle is known in the catch-as-catch-can style of wrestling as " *the hammer-lock with bar*," and it is of great value in promiscuous combat. It should be practised hundreds of times to acquire sureness and rapidity of execution, but I feel sure you will agree that it will be well worth the time spent on it.

A QUICK DEFENCE AGAINST A " BACK STRANGLE "

Your antagonist has caught you from behind, winding his *left* arm round your throat in a " garotte " or " back strangle." Bring your right elbow back viciously into his body. He is bound to wince, and so straightway bring your *right* hand up to his wrist and your *left* hand to his elbow, your fingers and thumbs being " on top " in each case.

Pull downwards and step backwards with your *right* foot, bringing it *outside* his *left*, and somewhat to his rear.

Withdraw your head from his arm, rendering this easy by increasing the downward pull on his wrist and forearm, and as soon as your head is free slip your right hand under his forearm and on to his upper arm, and you will have him securely " hammer-locked," as Fig. 42 on opposite page.

DEFENCE AGAINST A STICK ATTACK

If he should make a downward blow at your head with his left fist, a similar principle of defence can be followed out.

As the blow descends bring up your right arm, holding it rigidly to guard the blow with your forearm.

Follow this rapidly by swinging your *left* arm sharply upwards underneath his upper arm, and, bending your forearm well, bring your hand over the top of his *left* wrist. Your shoulder is brought close to him, and your *right* thumb is placed on his elbow as before.

Although he has his right hand free, he is unable to use it owing to the terrific pain existing in his left arm.

Here is yet another way of adapting the principle. You have got him on to the ground and are kneeling at his right side, your knees being well spread, the *left* at his armpit and the right against his hip. Lie across his body placing both forearms on the ground, your *left* elbow being drawn back against the side of his head.

Now with your *right* hand, take hold of his left wrist, and draw it upwards towards where your left hand is. Your left hand now takes the place of your right, grasping his wrist with your fingers on top. Now slip your *right* hand *under* his arm, and take hold of your own left wrist.

All that is needed now to apply the lock is for you to straighten your right arm, raising it upwards as you do so. If you drop your *forehead* on to his elbow you make the lock doubly secure. This is an easily obtained and extremely powerful " bent arm lock " that can be got at any time and from either side when you are on top of your adversary.

And yet one more :

He has thrown his left arm round your neck, whilst still facing you. If he hugs you close to him, it is to say the least, a most uncomfortable position.

Therefore, bring up your right hand to his elbow, placing the *palm* underneath and the thumb inside. Push his elbow upwards and outwards, bending your knees at the same time and his arm will be slipped over your head.

As this is happening, take his wrist (the left) in your left hand (fingers on top) and, continuing the " circular " lift on his elbow with your right hand, you will find that his body is twisted away from you. You have only to place his forearm over your right with the aid of your left hand and you again have the hammer lock (as Fig. 42, page 54).

CHAPTER XI

YOU HAVE A WEAPON IN YOUR BOOTS

There is one thing which everybody must get out of his mind—the idea that there are any rules whatsoever in modern warfare as the Nazis wage it. Actually, of course, warfare can be defined as a determined effort either to kill or so to disable the enemy as to eliminate him as a danger. And sometimes—the history of warfare on all sides is rich in such instances—it may be most inconvenient, most destructive of a plan of campaign, to deal as chivalrously with the enemy as one would wish. One must put him out of action—permanently if need be, or, alternatively, for such time as one has leisure to deal with him. It should be remembered that a dead gentleman is of no use to anybody except an undertaker ; that a live man, even though he may remain alive only by adopting the thug tactics which seem to come so easily to the enemy, remains an asset to his country. And we need every asset we possess.

Sketch A

This is an all-in war. There is no room for squeamishness. And in UNARMED COMBAT conducted ruthlessly, as it must be against a dangerous enemy, the *kick* can be extremely effective.

The normal way of kicking, of course, is to kick with the rear leg, or, alternatively, if one happens to be standing square, to take the leg back a little before flinging it forward. Such a method of

kicking, however, is rarely successful. It is too slow. The antagonist
can see it coming and usually finds
little difficulty either in getting out
of the way or else blocking the kick
with the sole of his boot. To essay
a kick in this style is comparable to
taking back the arm with a view to
delivering a punch, and thereby
advertising to your opponent your
intention.

The most effectual method of
disabling one's antagonist by a kick

Sketch B

is that brought to perfection by the Paris apache. It is known
as " La Savate," or, " Fighting with the feet." One most
disabling kick in the series involves stepping in close to your
adversary with, say, the right foot and chopping with the outer
edge of one's left boot right down the opponent's shin, from
just below the knee to the ankle (Sketch A). If, on the other
hand, it is more convenient or safer to step in closer to your
adversary with the left foot, then chop at his shin with the
inside of your right boot (Sketch B). This *chop kick*, properly
delivered, has an extremely damaging effect, since it invariably
lays open the whole shin and causes intense pain. It is also a
safe kick, for the turning movement of the body necessarily
involved in raising the leg to deliver the chop with the side of
the boot acts as a protection against a kick which may be
simultaneously delivered by your antagonist : this kick is
either blocked by the outside edge of the boot of your
" chopping leg," or, at worst, it finds its mark only on the
cheek of the buttocks, a fatty region where it is less uncom-
fortably absorbed than anywhere else on the body (see sketch).

Another kick in the La Savate series is a first-rate protection
against attack with a rifle butt or any other upraised weapon.
With this kick one does not make the mistake of taking the

Sketch C

leg back in order to swing it forward more powerfully. As has been emphasised that method is too slow. One delivers the kick by immediately, from the standing position, flinging the *foremost* foot forward and upward, with the toe pointed and the kicking leg held rigid. At the same time, in order to maintain balance and facilitate the movement, the knee of the standing leg is slightly bent. It will be appreciated that such a kick has all the advantages of surprise, for, since the foot travels the shortest possible distance, it can be delivered in a split second ; moreover, inasmuch as it is delivered from a standing position, the antagonist is not given notice (as with the preliminary withdrawal of the foot in the normal kick) of your intention. Directed at the fork of your antagonist's legs this kick can be completely disabling, and, at the very least, is always sufficiently disconcerting to the adversary to enable you to close with him, turn him, and put yourself in a safer position.

If you are in a really desperate situation, use your feet in one or other of the methods outlined.

If the reader has studied and practised the various methods of defence and attack outlined in this book, there is little doubt that he or she will be able to give a good account of themselves in almost any conditions except those, say, where the enemy, safely ensconsed under cover at a distance, is spraying the vicinity with machine gun bullets.

It has to be admitted, however, that even if you are within reach of the enemy, if that enemy happens to be armed with either rifle or revolver, he will present a slightly more difficult proposition. Even so, there is no need to despair. It is by no means an impossible feat to overcome an armed enemy without hurt to oneself. And if you have developed that confidence in yourself which it is one of the aims of this book to impart, there is no reason why you should not be successful.

WHEN YOU ARE HIS PRISONER

Presume that you are being poked along as a prisoner, with a rifle or other weapon thrust threateningly in your back. If you feel prepared to risk an attempt to turn the tables, whip round suddenly in one movement, at the same time bringing your arm with a scythe-like swing against the side of the rifle as you turn, dashing the weapon aside, the muzzle away from your body. Then step forward with the foot that is farthest away from the rifle, seize the enemy's arm and shoulder, and bring him down to the ground with that *back-chop* on the leg which has already been described. If the initial turning movement is executed with sufficient rapidity and smoothness, the enemy will have to be very alert to pull the trigger before the muzzle of his rifle has been thrust away from your body (see Sketches C and D).

THE ARMED MAN

Presume, again, that you are being held up with a rifle by an enemy who is facing you. Your hands as a consequence of the insistence of the enemy, are above your head, that individual being under the impression that you are less dangerous to him in that posture. Well, we shall see . . . Suddenly bring, say, your left arm down in a circular movement, knocking his rifle to one side away from your body. Then, almost simultaneously, a step forward will again place you in an advantageous position to execute the " *back chop*,"

Sketch D

Sketch E

the reverse back strangle or any of the turning movements (described in Chapter II) which are calculated to render the enemy hors-de-combat.

Another method of dealing with an enemy armed with a revolver and rifle—and one that is reasonably safe—is as follows :

Your enemy is facing you, holding his revolver or rifle in, say, his *right* hand. Knock aside the weapon with a swift circular movement of your *left* arm, and then quickly advance your right foot forward so that it is outside the enemy's *left* foot, dropping on your left knee as you do so. (See Sketch E.) Your *left* arm is now brought round back of his leg, your *left* hand coming against his shin or ankle and your shoulder and back being against the back of his knee (see illustration).

Now place your *right* hand over your *left* hand. Then pivoting on your *left* knee, bring your *left* foot inwards and throw all your weight backwards against his knee. Your hands will pull forward as your shoulder is thrown backwards, and the enemy will be brought down heavily on his face, with your

Sketch F

shoulder still making contact with the back of his knee (Sketches E and F).

Now push his *left* leg across the back of his *right*. Take hold of the right and pull it back towards him, thereby folding his left leg in the crook of his knee, as it were. Finally, spring on his back, and you will have the very secure and terrifically powerful cross-leg lock illustrated in Sketch G.

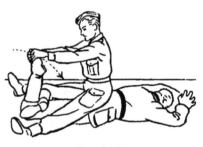

Sketch G

CHAPTER XII

SOME FINAL TIPS

In any sort of scuffle that begins when you are standing up, remember this : Always put yourself in safety by turning your antagonist, for by so doing you will give yourself time to consider your next move.

If, in a scuffle, you are on the ground, always endeavour to keep your legs around your adversary's body. By so doing you will restrict his movements and open the way to employing a neck or arm lock.

If, on the ground, the antagonist attempts to secure a scissors hold on you, do not be alarmed, even though your antagonist may be a powerful man. Just roll to a kneeling position and sit back, so to say, on your buttocks, making contact with your heels and lying flat against his body. This manœuvre alters the angle of attack and, as a consequence, the only pressure he can exert is against your hips, a fact which should cause you very little inconvenience. To escape altogether from this encircling hold place both hands on his groin and thrust down strongly, springing to your feet as you do so—but keeping the knees well bent. It should now be a quite simple matter to force his legs apart with your elbows and use your knee with effect against his crutch.

Do not forget that, in a desperate situation, attack is invariably the best defence. It is generally best to attack at the legs. If your antagonist is facing you, keep your eyes on his—always keep your eyes, if you can, on those of the opponent—and then, suddenly and without hesitation, bend forward and downward, gripping him about both legs. The moment you obtain your grip pull his legs *diagonally* forward, and even the strongest man will be brought flat on his back.

But under no circumstances pull your opponent *straight* forward, for such a movement makes it harder to upset his balance and may result, even though successful, in your being injured, by his boots or legs.

The diagonal thrust or pull is one of the most important essentials in unarmed combat. It is the application of the basic principle that a man without balance is without strength, and the diagonal thrust or pull is the easiest and surest way of putting an opponent off balance.

THINKING PHYSICALLY

This, then, is the art of Unarmed Combat. A knowledge of the series of physical movements outlined ; the training of the mind, by *thinking physically*, in initiating and carrying through those movements with rhythmic speed ; and the constant practice of the movements so that eventually they become automatic—performed without conscious thought ; those three requirements, which the student cannot help but acquire by intelligent application to his task, will place him in a position where he will have no reason to fear the outcome of any physical combat in which he may become engaged, whether with an invading enemy or merely with a home-grown tough. And even though no enemy may ever come within reach, though a serious affray with a thug may never occur, the student will find that the fact that he is equipped with the knowledge and skill to more than hold his own whatever may happen, will constitute a perpetual stiffening to his self-respect and his pride of manhood. In addition, of course, he will experience through the practice of the movements unarmed combat demands, an improvement in physical well-being and fitness of incalculable value both to himself and his country.